Iraq:
The Day After

Report of an Independent Task Force
Sponsored by the
Council on Foreign Relations

Thomas R. Pickering and James R. Schlesinger,
Co-Chairs
Eric P. Schwartz, Project Director

The Council on Foreign Relations is dedicated to increasing America's understanding of the world and contributing ideas to U.S. foreign policy. The Council accomplishes this mainly by promoting constructive debates and discussions, clarifying world issues, and publishing Foreign Affairs, the leading journal on global issues. The Council is host to the widest possible range of views, but an advocate of none, though its research fellows and Independent Task Forces do take policy positions.

THE COUNCIL TAKES NO INSTITUTIONAL POSITION ON POLICY ISSUES AND HAS NO AFFILIATION WITH THE U.S. GOVERNMENT. ALL STATEMENTS OF FACT AND EXPRESSIONS OF OPINION CONTAINED IN ALL ITS PUBLICATIONS ARE THE SOLE RESPONSIBILITY OF THE AUTHOR OR AUTHORS.

The Council will sponsor an Independent Task Force when (1) an issue of current and critical importance to U.S. foreign policy arises, and (2) it seems that a group diverse in backgrounds and perspectives may, nonetheless, be able to reach a meaningful consensus on a policy through private and nonpartisan deliberations. Typically, a Task Force meets between two and five times over a brief period to ensure the relevance of its work.

Upon reaching a conclusion, a Task Force issues a report, and the Council publishes its text and posts it on the Council website. Task Force reports can take three forms: (1) a strong and meaningful policy consensus, with Task Force members endorsing the general policy thrust and judgments reached by the group, though not necessarily every finding and recommendation; (2) a report stating the various policy positions, each as sharply and fairly as possible; or (3) a "Chairman's Report," where Task Force members who agree with the Chairman's report may associate themselves with it, while those who disagree may submit dissenting statements. Upon reaching a conclusion, a Task Force may also ask individuals who were not members of the Task Force to associate themselves with the Task Force report to enhance its impact. All Task Force reports "benchmark" their findings against current administration policy in order to make explicit areas of agreement and disagreement. The Task Force is solely responsible for its report. The Council takes no institutional position.

For further information about the Council or this Task Force, please write the Council on Foreign Relations, 58 East 68th Street, New York, NY 10021, or call the Director of Communications at (212) 434-9400. Visit our website at www.cfr.org.

TASK FORCE MEMBERS

CONTENTS

FOREWORD

War and peace have always been a continuum, no more so than today, no more so than in Iraq. In the aftermath of war, the nation-building and reconstruction process will be the responsibility of the U.S. government, other governments, international organizations, and nongovernmental organizations. But public policy schools and research centers also have an obligation to use their expertise to provide good information and ideas to those who might have to act.

With that in mind, the Council on Foreign Relations established a Task Force on the challenges of reconstruction and governance in a post-Saddam transition. These thoughts are embodied in this report.

This group follows the efforts of a joint study by the Council on Foreign Relations and the James A. Baker III Institute for Public Policy, *Guiding Principles for U.S. Post-Conflict Policy in Iraq*, published in January 2003. That report gives a good sense of the problems ahead, the context for both the problems and future policy, and an especially good discussion of specific issues such as energy.

This report relies heavily on the outstanding leadership of two of America's most outstanding foreign policy and national security figures: Dr. James R. Schlesinger, the former secretary of defense and energy; and Ambassador Thomas R. Pickering, the former U.S. ambassador to the United Nations and undersecretary of state. Eric P. Schwartz, a senior fellow at the Council, served as the most excellent project director. They assembled the team of leading experts to work with them, and they have worked exceedingly well.

In my words, not theirs, they make the following major points, backed with specific recommendations:

First, they urge President Bush to publicly explain America's and the world's vital interest in making Iraq a better and safer place. Further, the president must articulate to the American people why the United States must be prepared to stay the course to get that job done. Without that public commitment, Iraqis will certainly believe the United States and others will disappear on them before their lives are made better and safer; and American planners will never know where they stand and their effectiveness will be dissipated.

Second, they stress that the first priority on the ground in Iraq must go to prevent lawlessness and humanitarian suffering. Without public safety and a strong humanitarian aid program, nothing else will work.

Third, the United States must work very hard to involve the international community in the post-conflict transition and reconstruction effort, meaning shared responsibility and decision-making, without undercutting the unity of effort.

Fourth, the United States must make sure that plans and efforts are directed toward working with Iraqis in government, after proper vetting, to ensure continuing administration of public affairs and Iraqi responsibilities.

This report was first issued on March 12, 2003, shortly before the beginning of the war in Iraq. Events since that time have only served to validate and reaffirm the continuing relevance of the report's recommendations.

My great thanks go to James Schlesinger, Tom Pickering, and Eric Schwartz for their time, courage, great knowledge, and wisdom in pulling this report together so quickly and so well. Thanks also to Project Coordinator Colonel Martin Peatross, the Council's Marine Corps fellow. These folks have helped to make this report another in a continuing series of significant contributions to the national debate.

Leslie H. Gelb
President
Council on Foreign Relations

ACKNOWLEDGMENTS

In the aftermath of war in Iraq, the U.S. government will confront exceptionally challenging post-conflict transition and reconstruction issues. For these reasons, the Council on Foreign Relations was very fortunate that two distinguished Americans, Thomas R. Pickering and James R. Schlesinger, agreed to serve as co-chairs of the Task Force on Post-Conflict Iraq. Their experiences, perspectives, and willingness to devote considerable time and energy to this project were critical to the success of the overall effort.

I am very grateful to the members of the Task Force, who operated under very exacting time constraints. The Task Force includes specialists on the Middle East and the Persian Gulf, diplomatic and security issues, the rule of law and accountability, economics and energy, and post-conflict reconstruction, and the broad range of their contributions is reflected in this report. I would also like to thank retired Colonel Scott Feil and David Goldwyn for their advice on security and energy issues, respectively, and Council Senior Fellow Joseph Siegle for his contributions to the report's section on reconstruction.

The Task Force report builds on the excellent work of the Council on Foreign Relations–Baker Institute Working Group on Post-Conflict Iraq, which published *Guiding Principles for U.S. Post-Conflict Policy in Iraq* in January 2003. Rachel Bronson, who served as that project's co-director, provided the Task Force with important advice and assistance.

Colonel Martin D. Peatross, a Council military fellow, and Cheryl Igiri, a Council research associate, were instrumental in keeping the project on track. In addition to managing the publication schedule, Marty prepared draft sections relating to military and security issues, undertook research in a variety of areas, and served as our point of contact with the Council's executive office in New York City. Cheryl gathered and organized nearly all of the written research material for the project, responded quickly and effectively to a wide range of research inquiries, and ensured that the final document was in good order.

I would also like to thank Lee Feinstein, the deputy director of studies and director of strategic policy at the Council, for his guidance throughout this process. In addition, our work was strongly supported by Council staff, particularly Patricia Dorff, Anne Luzzatto, Lisa Shields, and Uday Ram.

The financial support of the Arthur Ross Foundation helped us move as quickly as the urgency of these issues demanded.

Finally, I want to thank Council President Leslie H. Gelb, who has strongly supported this project from the outset. I deeply appreciate his wise counsel, his commitment to the highest standards, and his conviction that our Iraq Task Force has an important role to play in the policy debate surrounding these critical issues.

Eric P. Schwartz
Project Director

EXECUTIVE SUMMARY

In a post-conflict Iraq, American interests will demand an extraordinary commitment of U.S. financial and personnel resources to transitional assistance and reconstruction. These interests include eliminating Iraqi weapons of mass destruction (WMD); ending Iraqi contacts, whether limited or extensive, with international terrorist organizations; ensuring that a post-transition Iraqi government can maintain the country's territorial integrity and independence while contributing to regional stability; and offering the people of Iraq a future in which they have a meaningful voice in the vital decisions that impact their lives.

But U.S. officials have yet to fully describe to Congress and the American people the magnitude of the resources that will be required to meet post-conflict needs. Nor have they outlined in detail their perspectives on the structure of post-conflict governance. The Task Force believes that these issues require immediate attention and encourages the administration to take action in four key areas:

Key Recommendation #1: An American political commitment to the future of Iraq. The president should build on his recent statements in support of U.S. engagement in Iraq by making clear to Congress, the American people, and the people of Iraq that the United States will stay the course. He should announce a multibillion-dollar, multiyear post-conflict reconstruction program and seek formal congressional endorsement. By announcing such a program, the president would give Iraqis confidence that the United States is committed to contribute meaningfully to the development of Iraq and would enable U.S. government agencies to plan more effectively for long-term U.S. involvement.

The scale of American resources that will be required could amount to some $20 billion per year for several years. This figure assumes a deployment of 75,000 troops for post-conflict peace stabilization (at about $16.8 billion annually), as well as funding for humanitarian and reconstruction assistance (as recommended immediately below). If the troop requirements are much larger than 75,000—a real possibility—the funding requirement would be much greater.

For reconstruction and humanitarian assistance alone, the president should request from Congress $3 billion for a one-year period and make clear that the United States will be prepared to make substantial additional contributions in the future. This initial contribution would include $2.5 billion for reconstruction and $500 million for humanitarian aid. (However, if there are significant interruptions in the availability of Iraqi oil revenues for use by the Oil for Food Program, the figure for humanitarian assistance would need to be considerably higher.)

Key Recommendation #2: Protecting Iraqi civilians—a key to winning the peace. From the outset of conflict, the U.S. military should deploy forces with a mission to establish public security and provide humanitarian aid. This is distinct from the tasks generally assigned to combat troops, but it will be critical to preventing lawlessness and reassuring Iraqis who might otherwise flee their homes. As women and children will constitute the majority of refugees and internally displaced persons, special efforts should be made to ensure that they are protected from sexual assault and that their medical and health needs are met. The Bush administration should sustain this public security focus throughout the transition. None of the other U.S. objectives in rebuilding Iraq would be realized in the absence of public security. If the administration fails to address this issue effectively, it will fuel the perception that the result of the U.S. intervention will be an increase in humanitarian suffering.

Additional recommendations—protecting Iraqi civilians:

- *Assist civilian victims of any use of WMD.* The U.S. and coalition partners should be ready to conduct rapid assessment of any use of weapons of mass destruction (WMD), publicize the results of such assessments, provide information to Iraqis on how to mitigate the impact of WMD, and provide assistance to alleviate the health effects of WMD exposure should it occur.

- *Seek to ensure protection for displaced persons and refugees.* Administration officials should press neighboring governments to provide safe haven in their countries for fleeing Iraqis. If the government of Turkey and other governments are determined to establish camps within the territory of Iraq, U.S. officials should seek to ensure that such camps are safe and secure.

- *Sustain, for the time being, the basic structure of the Oil for Food Program.* U.S. officials should work closely and intensively with the World Food Program (WFP) to ensure the continuation of the distribution network that sustains the Oil for Food Program. The program should be modified over time to ensure transparency and effectiveness in meeting Iraqi needs.

- *Actively recruit international civilian police (civpol) and constabulary forces.* Constabulary units such as Italy's carabinieri have equipment, training, and organization that enable them to maintain public order and address civil unrest. In addition, international civilian police could play an important role in vetting, training, and mentoring Iraqi police.

Key Recommendation #3: Sharing the burden for post-conflict transition and reconstruction. The Bush administration should move quickly to involve international organizations and other governments in the post-conflict transition and reconstruction process. This move will lighten the load on U.S. military and civilian personnel and help to diminish the impression that the United States seeks to control post-transition Iraq.

The Bush administration will likely be reluctant, especially early in the transition process, to sacrifice unity of command. On the other hand, other governments may be hesitant to participate in activities in which they have little responsibility. The Task Force recommends that the administration address this dilemma by promoting post-conflict Security Council resolutions that endorse U.S. leadership on security and interim civil administration in post-conflict Iraq, but also envision meaningful international participation and the sharing of responsibility for decision-making in important areas. The resolutions could direct the WFP or another international humanitarian organization to assume lead responsibility for humanitarian assistance (and involve nongovernmental organizations [NGOs] and Iraqi civil society in aid management and delivery); indicate that the United Nations (UN) will take responsibility in organizing (with U.S. support and assistance) the political consultative process leading to a transition to a new Iraqi government; establish an oil oversight board for Iraq; authorize the continuation of the UN's Oil for Food Program; establish a consortium of donors in conjunction with the World Bank and the International Monetary Fund (IMF) to consider Iraqi reconstruction needs as well as debt relief; and indicate that responsibilities in other areas could be transferred to the United Nations or other governments as conditions permit.

Key recommendation #4: Making Iraqis stakeholders throughout the transition process. The administration should ensure that Iraqis continue to play key roles in the administration of public institutions, subject to adequate vetting. Continuity of basic services will be essential and will require that thousands of Iraqi civil servants continue to do their jobs. In addition, every effort should be made quickly to establish Iraqi consultative mechanisms on political, constitutional, and legal issues, so that the period of interim governance will be limited and characterized by growing Iraqi responsibility on the political as well as administrative levels.

Additional recommendation—making Iraqis stakeholders:

- *Encourage a geographically based, federal system of government in Iraq.* In northern Iraq, the Kurdish population has operated outside of regime control for over a decade. While decisions on Iraq's constitutional structure should be made by Iraqis, the Task Force believes that a solution short of a federal system will risk conflict in a future Iraq, and that U.S. officials should adopt this perspective in their discussions with Iraqi counterparts and with Iraq's neighbors.

Other issues of concern to the Task Force include the following:

The rule of law and accountability. Police training must be supplemented by efforts to build other components of a system of justice, especially courts. The Task Force thus makes the following recommendations:

- *Deploy legal and judicial teams, and seek international involvement.* The administration should promote the post-conflict deployment of U.S. and international legal and judicial assistance teams to help address immediate and longer-term post-conflict justice issues.

- *Act early on accountability, seek international involvement in the process, and ensure a key role for Iraqis.* Given the enormity of human rights abuses by the regime, the Task Force believes that accountability issues should be an early priority for the transitional administration. International involvement in the process, through either the creation of an international ad hoc tribunal or the development of a mixed tribunal, will enhance the prospects for success. The Task Force notes that a truth and reconciliation process could be established concurrently with such a tribunal, as a complement to criminal accountability for those who bear greatest responsibility for abuses.

The Iraqi oil industry. U.S. officials will have to develop a posture on a range of questions relating to control of the oil industry, such as how decisions on contracts for equipment and oil-field rehabilitation will be made; who will consider and make judgments on the viability of executory contracts for development of oil fields (at least some of which have as a precondition the lifting of sanctions); and what will be required for transition from the Oil for Food Program to a transparent and accountable indigenous system to receive and disburse oil-related revenues.

The Task Force recommends that the administration strike a careful balance between the need to ensure that oil revenues benefit the people of Iraq and the importance of respecting the right of Iraqis to make decisions about their country's natural resources. In particular, the administration should undertake the following steps:

- *Emphasize publicly that the United States will respect and defend Iraqi ownership of the country's economic resources, especially oil; and seek an internationally sanctioned legal framework to assure a reliable flow of Iraqi oil and to reserve to a future Iraqi government the determination of Iraq's general oil policy.* The removal of the regime will not alter Iraqi obligations under the existing, UN-managed, legal framework for oil, but it will likely result in the need for modifications. The Task Force believes that a new framework, which could be affirmed by a Security Council resolution, could establish a decision-making oversight board with international and substantial Iraqi participation.

• *Address potential impact of regime change on Jordanian oil imports from Iraq.* The Iraqi regime has provided the government of Jordan with free and heavily discounted oil. It is unclear whether such arrangements would continue in the post-conflict environment. In view of Jordan's economic situation and its important role on regional and international security issues, the administration should make efforts to address Jordanian needs in this area.

Regional diplomatic and security issues. In the Persian Gulf region, U.S. officials will confront the challenge of effectively downsizing the Iraqi military while seeking to promote a longer-term security balance in which Iraq's territorial integrity can be maintained. In the Middle East, a successful U.S. and coalition intervention in Iraq will raise expectations about a new U.S. diplomatic initiative on the Arab-Israeli dispute. On these issues, the Task Force makes the following recommendations:

• *Closely monitor professionalization and restructuring of the Iraqi military, including disarmament, demobilization, and reintegration (DDR).* These tasks are likely to be carried out in large measure by private contractors or international development organizations and will require close supervision of what might otherwise be an uncoordinated effort. In addition, the Bush administration should promote programs in this area that emphasize civilian control of the military and respect for human rights.

- *Consider a regional forum for discussion of security issues.* The administration should strongly consider encouraging a security forum with states in the region. The forum could address confidence-building measures and related issues such as external security guarantees and nonproliferation.

- *Initiate post-conflict action on the Middle East peace process.* The Task Force encourages the administration to give high priority to an active, post-conflict effort to engage in the peace process and also believes that any such action by the administration must be accompanied by greater efforts by Arab states and the Palestinian leadership to discourage and condemn acts of terrorism and violence against Israelis and elsewhere in the region.

TASK FORCE REPORT

INTRODUCTION

In early March 2003, the United States was in the final stage of preparations for military action in Iraq. At that time, much official, media, and public attention had shifted to the security, governance, and reconstruction requirements in Iraq in the post-war period. By all accounts, those requirements will result in the deployment of many tens of thousands of U.S. troops, as well as the active engagement of U.S. civilian agencies involved in humanitarian assistance, law enforcement, judicial training, and economic assistance. This will represent an extraordinary commitment of financial and human resources.

The administration has strong reasons to make such a commitment, as the United States has vital interests that demand generous support of the post-conflict transition process. Those interests include eliminating Iraqi weapons of mass destruction (WMD); ending Iraqi contacts, whether limited or extensive, with international terrorist organizations; ensuring that a post-transition Iraqi government can maintain the country's territorial integrity and independence while contributing to regional stability; and offering the people of Iraq a meaningful voice in the vital decisions that impact their lives.

The Bush administration has recognized America's critical interests in ensuring that the post-conflict transition and reconstruction effort is no less successful than the military campaign. In a February 26 speech in Washington, President George W. Bush affirmed those interests, emphasizing that "rebuilding Iraq will require the sustained commitment from many nations, including our own." U.S. officials have also acknowledged that the United States, at least initially, will have to assume responsibility for a wide variety of immediate post-conflict requirements, from basic security for Iraqi civilians, to humanitarian assistance, to continuity of basic public services.

[8]

However, U.S. officials have yet fully to describe to Congress and the American people the magnitude of the resources that will be required to meet post-conflict needs. Nor have they outlined in detail their perspectives on the structure of post-conflict governance—and in particular, the roles of other governments, international organizations, and Iraqis themselves in civil administration, economic reconstruction, and the political transition to a new Iraqi government. The Task Force believes that these issues require urgent attention and encourages the Bush administration to take action in four key areas summarized directly below and described in greater detail in the body of this report.

An American political commitment to the future of Iraq. The president should build on his statements in support of U.S. engagement in Iraq by making clear to Congress, the American people, and the people of Iraq that the United States will stay the course. He should announce a multibillion-dollar, multiyear post-conflict reconstruction program and seek formal congressional endorsement. By announcing such a program, the president would give Iraqis confidence that the United States is committed to contributing meaningfully to the development of their country. The announcement would also enable U.S. government agencies to plan more effectively and ensure long-term U.S. engagement in Iraq even as U.S. officials turn their attention to other crises in the years to come.

President Bush has begun to explain to the American people the rationale for U.S. engagement in post-conflict Iraq. But he should intensify this effort and expand it to describe the scale of American resources that will be required, which may amount to some $20 billion per year for several years. This figure, which excludes the costs of fighting the war, assumes a deployment of 75,000 troops for post-conflict peace stabilization (estimated by the Congressional Budget Office at about $16.8 billion annually), as well as funding for humanitarian and reconstruction assistance. If, as many experts have suggested, the troop requirements are much larger than 75,000, the funding requirement would be much greater.

Protecting Iraqi civilians—a key to winning the peace. From the outset of conflict, the U.S. military should quickly deploy forces with a mission to establish public security and provide humanitarian aid. This is distinct from the tasks generally assigned to combat troops but will be critical to preventing lawlessness and reassuring Iraqis who might otherwise flee their homes. The Bush administration must sustain this public security focus throughout the transition. None of the other U.S. objectives in rebuilding Iraq will be realized in the absence of public security.

Many Iraqi civilians will be at serious risk if U.S. troops do not maintain a substantial ground presence and a public security focus in areas under U.S. and coalition control, and in areas simply abandoned by Iraqi forces. As women and children will constitute the majority of refugees and internally displaced persons, special efforts should be made to ensure that they are protected from sexual assault and that their medical and health care needs are met. If the administration fails to address the public security issue effectively, it would allow the perception to grow that the result of the U.S. intervention will be an increase in humanitarian suffering.

The Bush administration should take a range of additional actions to promote public security in Iraq during the post-conflict transition period and to reform and reestablish Iraqi capacities in this area. In particular, U.S. officials should be actively engaged with other governments in developing a "public security and justice package" for Iraq, which would include international civilian police who could vet, train, and monitor Iraqi law enforcement personnel. The package would also include legal and judicial assistance.

Sharing the burden for post-conflict transition and reconstruction. The administration should move quickly to involve international organizations and other governments in the post-conflict transition and reconstruction process. This move will lighten the load on U.S. military and civilian personnel and capitalize on the considerable expertise of other governments in law enforcement training, judicial and legal reform, and military training. It will also help to diminish the impression that the United States seeks to control post-transition Iraq. The sharing of responsibility with others, which may be necessary to secure their involvement, can be accomplished without sacrificing unity of effort.

To be sure, there will likely be a U.S. reluctance, especially early in the transition process, to sacrifice unity of command. The Task Force recommends that the Bush administration seek to address this dilemma by promoting post-conflict United Nations (UN) Security Council resolutions that endorse U.S. leadership on security and an interim civil administration in post-conflict Iraq, but also envision that the United Nations and other international organizations take responsibility for issues such as management of humanitarian assistance, the political consultative process leading to a new Iraqi government, the UN-supervised Oil for Food Program, and reconstruction.

Make Iraqis stakeholders throughout the transition process. The administration should ensure that Iraqis continue to play key roles in the administration of government institutions, subject to adequate vetting. In addition, every effort should be made quickly to establish Iraqi consultative mechanisms on political, constitutional, and legal issues, so that the period of interim governance will be limited and characterized by growing Iraqi responsibility on political as well as administrative levels.

In a speech to the Council on Foreign Relations in February 2003, Stephen Hadley, the deputy assistant to the president for national security affairs, said, "We will draw free Iraqis into the task of rebuilding Iraq from the outset and transfer responsibilities to Iraqi entities as soon as possible." The Task Force believes it will be critical to implement the approach outlined by Hadley. In the first instance, this means that Iraqi civil servants should continue to play a role in managing public institutions. It also means that non-Iraqis who are put into senior management positions should take advantage of existing local expertise and seek to transfer responsibilities to Iraqi citizens as promptly as conditions will permit. Over time, a continued presence of large numbers of non-Iraqi leaders in the institutions of governance would foster alienation and resentment.

To be sure, the absence of non-compromised political institutions and the uncertain public security environment in Iraq will make it extremely difficult to attempt an immediate post-conflict transfer to an Iraqi-led central government. At the same time, Iraqis have highly developed technical capacities in areas relating to public services and management. They should be deeply involved both in transitional governance and the political transition process.

Although the four issues described above represent what the Task Force believes should be key areas of attention for U.S. policymakers, we publish this report with an awareness that the United States and coalition partners will face enormous uncertainty in the post-conflict environment. In fact, it is impossible to predict with confidence which issues will emerge as the most serious obstacles to U.S. objectives. The administration will have to undertake this post-conflict effort with considerable modesty and an understanding that any plans will be continually modified. For this reason, many of the Task Force's recommendations reflect the importance of planning for a wide range of contingencies, as well as the value of flexibility in on-the-ground response.

A note on methodology and scope: The Task Force report was written at a time when the post-conflict planning process was well underway, and generally reflects information available as of early March 2003. We have sought to avoid recommendations on issues where U.S. intentions were unambiguous, where there was broad and unquestioned consensus, and where a nongovernmental task force offered little comparative advantage. Thus, we have not found it necessary to urge the U.S. military to seek quickly to identify WMD sites or to protect oil fields—critical objectives that have been a central part of military planning for many months. Nor do we presume to offer tactical advice on how best to accomplish these goals. Rather, we have sought to identify important policy challenges in areas where final decisions have yet to be made; to describe the official planning that has taken place in these areas; and to offer recommendations about the best way forward.

The Task Force project is based on the view that the United States should be in the best possible position to respond to post-conflict challenges. At the same time, there are varying perspectives on whether the use of force was necessary to compel Iraqi compliance with relevant Security Council resolutions. The endorsement of the conclusions of this report by Task Force members does not imply any position on the question of going to war in Iraq.

Task Force Report

HUMANITARIAN ISSUES

Assessing the Challenge
Providing food, shelter, medicine, and other critical requirements
after the outbreak of hostilities, and in the immediate aftermath
of conflict, will be a significant challenge. The Fourth Geneva Con-
vention requires that the United States seek to ensure a broad range
of humanitarian protections for Iraqi civilians in the context of armed
conflict and its aftermath. Beyond this legal requirement, U.S. military and civilian officials have keen humanitarian and political
interests in ensuring that basic food, clothing, shelter, and security needs are met. Failure to address this issue effectively would
fuel the impression, within the region and around the world,
that an intervention has caused an increase in the humanitarian
suffering of the Iraqi people.

The magnitude of this challenge will be affected by both the
duration and the nature of the conflict. If U.S. and coalition forces
face little or no resistance, if major hostilities in most areas of the
country are over in a matter of days, and if Iraqi forces do not attack
Iraqi civilians with chemical or biological weapons, conditions will
likely permit rapid entry of relief officials and maintenance of pre-
existing food delivery infrastructure. On the other hand, a more
protracted conflict—especially if it involves extended urban war-
fare, oil-field destruction, or use of chemical or biological weapons—
will increase the risk of severe humanitarian suffering.

One cause of concern during the conflict will be the public-
security situation in areas abandoned by Iraqi security forces.
During conflict, in the absence of a U.S. or coalition troop presence, there will be potential for reprisals and lawlessness. In addition, there are justified concerns about forced movements of
civilians. UN officials have estimated that some 1.45 million Iraqis
could flee into Turkey, Iran, Jordan, Syria, and Kuwait, and that
war could result in the internal displacement of an additional 900,000
Iraqis. These numbers compound estimates of up to 1.1 million
Iraqis who are already internally displaced, as well as many hundreds of thousands who are living as refugees in neighboring
countries.

The nature of the coalition's military intervention could also have significant implications for population movements. In particular, in areas of heavy Shi'a population in the south and in parts of Baghdad, as well as in Kurdish areas in the north, a very early and substantial presence of coalition ground troops may be necessary to avert regime attempts to sow discord or encourage flight. In addition, an early coalition presence in the north may help to allay concerns (and diminish the prospects of flight) on the part of the Kurdish population.

Given the possibility of efforts by Iraqis to cross borders, much attention has focused on the preparation and the willingness of neighboring governments to provide refuge to asylum-seekers. Iran has indicated that it will provide safe haven to Iraqis and has readied camps along its western border. Turkey seems less forthcoming, with indications that Ankara plans to establish camps within northern Iraq. (Moreover, U.S.-Turkish diplomacy on this issue has been complicated by the U.S. desire to obtain Turkish agreement to a U.S. troop presence.) Even if the period of hostilities is short, displaced-persons camps inside Iraq raise significant challenges, especially given the possible post-conflict lack of stability in the north. In short, internal camps that lack adequate protection and humane and efficient management are not good substitutes for refuge outside the country of origin.

A prolonged conflict will expose the relatively fragile condition of the Iraqi population. In terms of access to food, clean water, and medicine, as well as their general economic situation, Iraqis are in a more difficult position in 2003 than they were in 1991. Today, some 16 million Iraqis, or about 60 percent of the population, rely on food rations from the UN's Oil for Food Program. While the program is implemented by UN officials in the northern areas outside of government control, that is not the case in the central and southern parts of the country, where a network of some 43,000 Iraqi personnel distribute food rations.

Status of Planning

U.S. military planners appear to anticipate that the U.S. military will have to assume the bulk of responsibility for the initial humanitarian response during the conflict and in its immediate aftermath. While this may well include securing access to potable water, delivery of food, and provision of basic health services, the more critical requirement is likely to be the maintenance of public security. There have reportedly been some consultations between the U.S. military and the U.S. Agency for International Development (USAID) on how to avoid acts of reprisal in the aftermath of conflict. At the same time, it is uncertain whether U.S. troops involved in combat operations will be in a position to focus, in a systematic manner, on the prevention of reprisals and other threats to civilians.

As of late February, plans for the organization and management of an overall post-conflict relief effort were still being made. A new Pentagon Office of Reconstruction and Humanitarian Assistance, established pursuant to a National Security Presidential Directive and described in greater detail below, will have overall responsibility for the coordination of post-conflict activities, including humanitarian aid. That office has begun discussions with international organizations and foreign governments on their potential contributions to the relief effort.

The new Pentagon office will rely heavily on USAID's Office of Foreign Disaster Assistance, which intends to deploy dozens of disaster assistance response team (DART) officers to Iraq. They would deploy with civil affairs personnel from the military as soon as conditions permit their entry and would reportedly identify needs relating largely to displaced persons in the north and border areas. At least for the duration of the conflict, their movements would be limited, and they would probably not have extensive access to other areas of the country.

The involvement of international relief organizations will be substantial. In particular, the UN High Commissioner for Refugees (UNHCR) has been working with governments in the region to equip refugee camps for Iraqis who cross borders and the World Food Program (WFP) has been stockpiling food in the region. However, agencies reported severe funding shortages, indicating that only about $30 million of a $120 million planning requirement had been raised, as of mid-February.

Recommendations

- *Promptly establish a ground presence in areas of likely refugee flight.* In the southern areas of Iraq, such as Karbala and Najaf, as well as in Kurdish areas in the north, all efforts should be made to establish an early presence of U.S. ground troops, which may be necessary to avoid Iraqi actions to sow discord and encourage flight. A rapid presence in the north would also address Kurdish concerns about the intentions of Turkish forces (although such a presence would be made more challenging if Turkey refuses to grant U.S. troops access to Iraq from its bases).

- *Maintain sufficient follow-on forces for public security.* During the conflict, in areas already under the control of coalition forces, U.S. military officials should deploy follow-on and support forces to establish public security and provide essential humanitarian needs. (Stabilization forces should also be deployed to areas that are simply abandoned by the Iraqi military.) As women and children will constitute the majority of internally displaced persons, special efforts should be made to ensure that they are protected from sexual assault and that their medical and health care needs are met.

- *Make rapid assessment of the impact of any WMD use.* The U.S. military should be prepared to conduct rapid assessments of any use of WMD and to publicize the results of such assessments so that Iraqis can make informed decisions. In the absence of such a concerted effort, the use of WMD—or rumors of such use—would result in large-scale population movements. Similar assessments should be made about the dangers to civilians from oil-field destruction and extended urban combat.

- *Plan to assist civilian victims of any WMD use.* There is very limited U.S. military capability to respond to widespread WMD attacks on civilians by the Iraqi regime. Nonetheless, the United States and coalition partners should plan to provide as much assistance as possible should such attacks occur, or should toxins be released as a result of an inadvertent strike on a WMD facility. These efforts should include U.S. requests for assistance from other governments with expertise in this area (such as those from the former Warsaw Pact). In addition, the United States, possibly in conjunction with others, should prepare information for wide distribution to Iraqis on how civilians can mitigate the impact of WMD use.

- *Seek to ensure protection for displaced persons and refugees.* Administration officials should press neighboring governments to provide refuge in their countries for fleeing Iraqis. However, if Turkey and other governments are determined to establish camps within the territory of Iraq, U.S. officials should ensure that such camps are safe and secure. This effort could be accomplished by stationing U.S. military liaison officers in such facilities and deploying civilian administrators and monitors in the camps.

- *Sustain, for the time being, the basic structure of the Oil for Food Program.* U.S. officials should work closely and intensively with the World Food Program to ensure the continuation of the distribution network that sustains the Oil for Food Program. In the first instance, the WFP is reportedly planning to utilize the existing network of food distribution agents in the aftermath of conflict. U.S. officials should support these plans, support possible use of additional personnel to assist in food distribution should the existing structure break down, and offer both logistical and personnel assistance on an urgent basis to sustain the program in the aftermath of conflict.

- *Encourage internationalization of humanitarian assistance.* U.S. officials should not "own" the humanitarian assistance effort, as strong international participation will enhance the likelihood of international burden-sharing and communicate to Iraqis, as well as to other states within the region, that the aid effort is broadly supported. Moreover, organizations such as the WFP and UNHCR will be deeply engaged in Iraq, and donors may be more likely to fund their operations if overall management is not the responsibility of one government. Finally, many humanitarian assistance questions involve technical and logistical rather than political and security issues, diminishing the potential that a handoff of responsibilities will complicate U.S. policymaking. At the earliest opportunity, U.S. officials should engage in discussions with other governments, voluntary agencies, and the UN Secretariat about the early handoff of responsibility for humanitarian operations. Such a transfer could be endorsed by a Security Council resolution.

STRUCTURE OF POST-CONFLICT TRANSITIONAL ADMINISTRATION

Background

Why transitional administration? The defeat of the Iraqi regime will leave a vacuum of political authority in the country, and Iraq will require interim institutions to exercise authority in areas of governance that include public security, civil administration, and reconstruction and development. While some have argued for a quick, or even immediate, transfer of sovereignty to Iraqis, post-conflict conditions would make such a course of action extremely difficult to implement. First, there is a distinct dearth of non–Ba'ath Party political institutions or leaders who could quickly establish political legitimacy. As one Task Force member indicated during our deliberations, "Iraqi society has been decapitated. Those of real stature have been forced out of the country, forced underground, or killed." To be sure, there are local figures with some stature, including some tribal and religious leaders, and those with some prominence who pre-date the current regime. Moreover, U.S. policy should strongly encourage the emergence of indigenous leadership. However, the broad popularity of these local figures has yet to be tested, and they likely have limited or no experience in governance.

The Task Force believes that opposition leaders who have lived outside the country have an important role to play in the political future of Iraq. However, it would be inappropriate, at best, and counterproductive, at worst, to establish a transitional administration

[18]

in which such figures exercise exclusive, sovereign authority. Imposition of such a transitional arrangement would be undemocratic and could alienate large segments of the Iraqi population.

The post-conflict security environment will also be incompatible with the immediate reintroduction of indigenous authority. With the expected defeat of the Iraqi army, U.S. and allied forces will have to assume responsibility for both internal and external security. With respect to the former, the risks of continued conflict are significant. For example, Kurds in the north who were forcibly displaced by the regime from cities such as Kirkuk may seek to return to homes now occupied by Iraqis who relocated from the center of the country. And in southern Shi'a areas and other parts of Iraq, individuals and groups who had been repressed may attempt reprisals against Ba'ath Party officials and other senior figures in the regime.

Iraq's neighbors will also have stakes in these internal security issues, creating additional security challenges that could impact a post-war transitional authority. According to reports in early 2003, some Turkish troops were already in northern Iraq, and it is widely believed that the Turkish troop presence could expand with the advent of war (with or without a U.S.-Turkish agreement on U.S. deployments in Turkey). Should Turkish officials believe that post-war internal conflict threatens members of the Turkoman community in Iraq, or that Kurdish politicians are seeking to realize Kurdish political ambitions in ways inimical to Turkish interests, they could be inclined to have Turkish troops play a more active role in the north. This, in turn, might result in greater involvement by Iran, which sees itself as a defender of Shi'a interests in Iraq.

Despite these factors, there is good reason to believe that even if Iraqis themselves do not have immediate authority for transitional governance, they could play an important role in the administering of government institutions during a transitional period, subject to adequate vetting. There is also reason to believe that the period of interim governance could be relatively limited in duration, and characterized by growing Iraqi responsibilities on the political and administrative levels. In contrast to the populations in many other post-conflict societies, Iraqi men and women are well educated and have highly developed technical capacity in areas such as public services and management.

Options for transitional administration. As described in the section on status of planning (below), the Bush administration has already decided that the transitional administration in Iraq will, at least initially, be under the authority of U.S. Combatant Commander General Tommy Franks. At the same time, a range of important related issues have yet to be considered, and assessment of these issues requires a brief description of general organizational issues in this area.

In recent years, the international community has adopted several forms of transitional administration in post-conflict societies, and, in most cases, the arrangements for security have differed from those for civil administration. In almost all recent post-conflict situations where peace enforcement—that is, the consistent application of military force to compel compliance—remained a major requirement, a coalition of like-minded states, in some cases with one state in the lead, has taken on the bulk of responsibility for external and, at least in the initial stages, internal security. In East Timor, for example, that responsibility was assumed by the Australian-led InterFET operation. In Bosnia and Kosovo, North Atlantic Treaty Organization (NATO) forces provided security; and in Afghanistan, that responsibility is in the hands of the International Security Assistance Force (now led by Germany), with the support of U.S. combat forces. While all of these operations were authorized by the UN Security Council, none were "blue-helmeted," or under UN operational control. All were "green-helmeted coalitions of the willing," and it is widely recognized that traditional, blue-helmeted peacekeeping forces are not well equipped for the demands of peace enforcement.

In a range of peace enforcement operations composed of green-helmeted military forces, international organizations and governments have effectively deployed civilian police, police monitors, and police trainers to provide public security and law enforcement. Such deployments address a law enforcement gap that military forces are not ideally equipped to fill. U.S. military leaders, in particular, are reluctant to assume long-term responsibility for public security and have traditionally argued that transitional civilian policing and police training should be undertaken by others. In Iraq, international civilian police (civpol) personnel could play an important role, as police reform will be a critical objective.

In the area of transitional civilian administration, there is a range of possible options. These include (but are not limited to) a civilian administrator operating under the authority of a military commander (the option that was apparently chosen by the president); rule by a civilian administrator who is effectively responsible to the occupying power or to a coalition of governments; and rule by a civilian administrator acting through the authority of a regional or international organization such as the United Nations. Each of these alternatives could include (or be followed by) a transfer of sovereign authority to an indigenous interim regime. Under any of these options, there are advantages to international legal action—such as a resolution by the UN Security Council—to endorse the transitional arrangement. It would, of course, be necessary to convince the Security Council to accept such a resolution in a form that the United States would favor, which is certainly not a foregone conclusion at this stage. And of course, the U.S. task would be complicated further if the Security Council does not endorse—or at least acquiesce in—a U.S. decision to use force in Iraq.[1]

Despite these obstacles, trying to obtain such an endorsement might still be worthwhile, as a resolution could increase the likelihood of international involvement and financial and other support for reconstruction in the post-conflict environment. It is worth noting that the interim administration will be compelled to make decisions on a progressively broader range of political, economic, and social issues over time. Without additional international sanction, the basic authority for such decisions could be limited to the international law of occupation. However flexible that law may be, a broader international endorsement of the transitional administration could have significant political benefits.

---

[1]On the other hand, there might be sympathy for U.S. efforts if post-conflict investigations revealed widespread Iraqi violations of Security Council resolutions relating to weapons of mass destruction.

Status of Planning

As of late February, the Bush administration had indicated that the U.S. combatant commander would have ultimate authority in a post-conflict Iraq. The administration also intended to name a U.S. civilian administrator, under the authority of the combatant commander, with responsibility for transitional civil administration, humanitarian assistance, and reconstruction. U.S. officials envisioned making use of current Iraqi administrative personnel to the largest extent possible. In testimony before the Senate Foreign Relations Committee, Undersecretary of Defense Douglas Feith indicated that "major Iraqi governmental institutions, such as government ministries, could remain and perform the key functions of government after the vetting of top personnel."

The administration also reportedly plans to form an Iraqi political or consultative council to advise the civilian administrator, a judicial council to advise on law revisions, and a constitutional commission to draft a new constitution.[2] Members of the two councils and the constitutional commission would come from the émigré opposition and from within Iraq. U.S. officials also have indicated that once the security situation in Iraq is stabilized, the U.S. civil administrator might be removed from the military chain of command. Officials have not indicated precisely to whom in the civilian leadership the civil administrator would then report.

This structure is consistent with a National Security Presidential Directive issued by President Bush in late January, in which the president placed responsibility for post-conflict rebuilding of Iraq within the U.S. Department of Defense. The department has established an Office of Reconstruction and Humanitarian Assistance for Iraq, under the leadership of retired lieutenant general Jay Garner. Garner, who commanded one of the U.S. military's joint task forces in support of Operation Provide Comfort in northern

---

[2]The administration has not yet announced its position on the applicable governing law for Iraq during a transition period, although it is expected that Iraqi law, up to a specified date, may serve as the basis for transitional legal arrangements. Of course, a decision on this issue should involve extensive consultation with Iraqis.

Iraq, is expected to serve as the civilian administrator in Iraq for an initial period. He is still building his staff, which is reportedly expected to have some 200 members divided into four functional groups. These include 1) humanitarian assistance, 2) civil administration, 3) reconstruction coordination, and 4) operational support (with responsibilities for managing logistics and military-related peace stabilization activities, such as restructuring the Iraqi army).[3] General Garner's operation, or at least significant components of it, is expected to deploy to Iraq shortly after hostilities end.

These efforts complement and incorporate various administration planning processes, including the State Department's "Future of Iraq Project," announced in March 2002. With the involvement of Iraqis in the opposition exile movement, the administration developed seventeen working groups dealing with issues such as transitional justice; public finance; democratic principles; public health and humanitarian issues; public outreach; water, agriculture, and the environment; economy and infrastructure; local government; defense policy; oil and energy; education; anti-corruption; civil-society capacity-building; building a free media; return of refugees and displaced persons; foreign policy; and preserving Iraq's cultural heritage. While some of these groups have been more active than others (in fact, some groups have been largely inactive), the project initiated technical plans in a number of important areas. For example, Iraqi lawyers working on the project have drafted hundreds of pages of proposed reforms of key Iraqi legislation, as well as proposals for reform of the police, the courts, and the prisons.

The key challenge will be to transform these activities into a coherent and unified effort and to ensure that policy formulated in Washington is accepted internationally and effectively implemented in Iraq. As of late February 2003, administration officials acknowledged that they were just beginning to address these coordination and implementation issues.

---

[3] As of late February, however, this structure was reportedly under review, with the possibility of changes being made.

If effectively implemented, the main advantage of this Department of Defense–led structure for post-war governance in Iraq is that it will provide clear responsibility and an accountable chain of command: from the president to the secretary of defense, to the combatant commander and the civilian administrator. This could be an improvement over more dispersed responsibility for stabilization efforts that has characterized other post-conflict operations, most recently in Afghanistan. At the same time, other U.S. agencies, other governments, and international organizations, whose involvement and participation may be key to the success of the post-conflict endeavor, will have less authority, may feel less responsibility for the results, and thus may be less engaged in the process. More importantly, other governments and international organizations may be uncomfortable with putting their civilian assets—such as police, judges, and civil administrators—under U.S. government control. The recommendation offered below attempts to address this challenge.

Recommendation
Strengthen transitional administration by facilitating the participation of other governments and international organizations in a range of post-conflict activities. The United States will want other governments and international organizations to provide personnel and financial support to transitional administration and post-conflict peace-building in Iraq. In particular, the administration will want to lighten the load on U.S. military and civilian personnel over time by taking advantage of European and other international expertise in law enforcement, judicial and constitutional reform, and military and police training, among other areas. In addition, international involvement will help to diminish the impression that the United States seeks to control post-transition Iraq. While the prospect of sharing responsibilities for a transitional administration might serve as an incentive for the involvement of international organizations and foreign governments, there will likely be a U.S. reluctance, especially early in the transition process, to sacrifice unity of command. The Task Force recommends that the administration seek to address this dilemma by promoting post-

conflict Security Council resolutions that endorse U.S. leadership on security and interim civil administration in post-conflict Iraq, but that it also envision meaningful international participation and responsibility-sharing in ways that will enhance the credibility of the transition effort. In particular, the resolutions could

- Direct the WFP or another international humanitarian organization to take responsibility for humanitarian assistance to Iraqis;

- Indicate that the United Nations will take responsibility in organizing (with U.S. support and assistance) the consultative process that will lead to a political transition to Iraqi rule;

- Establish an oil oversight board, with Iraqi and international participation;

- Authorize the continuation of the UN-supervised Oil for Food Program, albeit in a modified form;

- Establish a consortium of donors, in conjunction with the World Bank and the IMF, to consider Iraqi reconstruction needs as well as debt relief; and

- Indicate that responsibilities in other areas of transitional assistance could be further transferred to the United Nations or other governments as conditions permit.

KEY ISSUES IN TRANSITIONAL ADMINISTRATION

Public Security and Law Enforcement

Background
It is clear that public security in the immediate aftermath of an intervention will be the responsibility of coalition forces, both as a matter of international law and as a matter of necessity. The challenge will be formidable, especially during the period of war and its immediate aftermath. Even after the regime is defeated and a civilian police structure begins to re-emerge, military forces will still have to play a supporting, constabulary role to address situations that go beyond the capabilities of local police.

It is difficult to know how many U.S. troops should be devoted to public security activities in post-conflict Iraq. For example, historical experience provides only limited guidance, as per capita troop numbers have varied widely in post-conflict environments from the Balkans to Afghanistan. One respected military analyst, retired Colonel Scott R. Feil of the Association of the U.S. Army, has suggested that a force of about 75,000 U.S. troops for about one year will be the minimum required to stabilize the situation and accomplish critical tasks related to post-conflict security, transitional assistance, and civil administration.[4] These include, inter alia, protection of key strategic areas, ensuring disarmament of Iraqi forces, destruction of WMD, core security in the largest cities and key outlying areas, support for the humanitarian effort, and border patrol. Other analysts have suggested the number may be far higher, but few have argued that the 75,000 figure is too low. For example, General Eric Shinseki, chief of staff of the army, recently suggested to members of Congress that the requirement could be several hundred thousand troops, though Deputy Secretary of Defense Paul Wolfowitz subsequently challenged General Shinseki's estimate as "way off the mark."

The regime's special security organizations will need to be disbanded, with their members subject to vetting. In addition, the leadership of forces performing day-to-day law enforcement—which may total some 70,000 people from the national police force and the frontier guard—will have to be removed. At the same time, it is expected that these law enforcement groups could remain intact, subject to active monitoring and supervision. It has been estimated that these supervision and monitoring tasks, if not performed by the militaries of coalition members, could require between 4,000 and 5,000 international civilian police.[5]

---

[4]Scott R. Feil's testimony from the Senate Foreign Relations Committee hearing on "Reconstruction of Post-Saddam Iraq," August 1, 2002.

[5]Feil's testimony from the Senate Foreign Relations Committee hearing on "Security in a Post-Conflict Situation in Iraq," February 11, 2003, p. 1. See also Robert M. Perito, "Establishing Post-Conflict Security and the Rule of Law in Iraq," United States Institute of Peace, February 2003, p. 24.

Status of Planning

The U.S. Central Command has been planning for this broad public security requirement, which will, in the initial stages at least, include activities normally assigned to police. In addition, the administration has begun to consider options for deployment of civpol from the United States and other countries. However, detailed plans have yet to be developed.

Recommendations

- *Robust military deployment for public security.* While it is not possible to know the first-year requirements for peace stabilization troops, the Task Force notes that estimates have ranged from about 75,000 to more than 200,000. The Task Force recommends that deployments for peace stabilization err on the side of robustness. In all post-conflict situations, and especially in Iraq, the critical enabling condition for post-conflict reconstruction is security, and Iraqi police will not quickly be in a position to fill the law-and-order vacuum.

- *Actively recruit civpol and constabulary forces.* Ultimately, the Bush administration should not rely solely on U.S. soldiers to perform police duties and police monitoring. Other governments have developed forces that have characteristics of both the military and the police, and they can play a valuable role in support of law enforcement in post-conflict situations. Units such as Italy's carabinieri have equipment, training, and organization that enable them to fight as light infantry but also to maintain public order and address civil unrest. In addition, a range of regional and international organizations have developed capabilities for recruitment and deployment of international civilian police.[6] The Task Force urges that the administration work with other governments, as well as regional and international organizations—such as the European Union (EU), the Organization for Security and Cooperation in Europe (OSCE), and the United Nations—in recruiting national constabulary

---

[6]See Perito, "Establishing Post-Conflict Security," pp. 18–21, for a discussion of constabulary forces.

units as well as international civilian police. That effort should begin now, and the organizations should ideally be in place to follow the combat forces into Iraq. Finally, it will be important to ensure that women are included in international civilian police, and to provide training relating to gender-based violence, as has been done in other post-conflict environments.

The Political Constituting Mechanism for the Future of Iraq

Background

A statement by a coalition of Iraqi opposition figures, in their Democratic Principles Working Group report of November 2002, describes the basic challenge in charting a political future for the people of Iraq:

> As a result [of the oppressive rule of Saddam Hussein], there are no recognized domestic political institutions, groups or individuals that can step forward, invoke national legitimacy and assume power. A political vacuum will arise during the period of disintegration and following the downfall of the regime. Many groups and individuals will eventually emerge and compete for power, but this will only happen gradually, as the environment becomes safe for public participation.[7]

This challenge is compounded by the fact that Ba'ath Party policies have accentuated ethnic and religious differences within Iraq. While we should not assume that such differences present insurmountable obstacles to a successful political transition, the actions of the regime have complicated efforts to establish a political process that integrates and unites the people of the country. The Kurdish population in the north, which already enjoys substantial autonomy, has been subjected to mass killings, forced relocation, and other abuses, and will harbor understandable concerns about a constitutional process that might result in a diminution of its political authority. At the same time, Shi'a populations in southern Iraq have been subjected to severe violations of their civil

---

[7]"Final Report on the Transition to Democracy in Iraq," Democratic Principles Working Group, November 2002, p. 16.

and political rights at the hands of the regime, as have other aggrieved communities such as Assyrians and Turkomen.

Under these conditions the civilian administration will have to consider the nature of the political constituting process—that is, the process by which the people of Iraq establish the constitutional system that will dictate their political future. Key issues include the timing of any process, the manner in which representatives are chosen for any consultation that precedes elections, and the basic rules for decision-making in a consultative process. Finally, whatever decisions are made, U.S. officials will need to consider the value of international involvement and endorsement of the political constituting process, such as through a UN Security Council resolution. Such action would help to ensure that the overall effort is accepted not only internationally, but within the region and by all of the population groups within Iraq.

Status of Planning
U.S. officials have not publicly detailed their plans for the political constituting process; in fact such plans are still being developed. In testimony in mid-February 2003, Undersecretary of Defense Feith acknowledged that "the issue [of] how a transition would occur is not knowable precisely right now." At the same time, and as mentioned above, elements that the administration appears to be considering include an Iraqi political or consultative council, a judicial council to work on law revision, and a constitutional commission to draft a new constitution.

The Bush administration has also given some indications of the kind of political system it would like to see emerge in Iraq, although it has not spelled out its preferences in detail. For example, Undersecretary Feith, in testimony before the Senate Foreign Relations Committee, spoke about the efforts of the Iraqi National Congress (INC), a political umbrella organization for Iraqi opposition founded in 1992, to organize conferences of "multiple groups" of Iraqi oppositionists in recent years. Undersecretary Feith indicated that those conferences have "promulgated principles that all of the major Iraqi oppositions now subscribe to that are principles that we support [sic]." The principles to which

Undersecretary Feith was apparently referring were first expressed in a political declaration at an October 1992 conference of the INC at Salahuddin, in northern Iraq. In sum, the declaration called for a democratic and federally structured Iraq, based on the principles of separation of powers and protection of both individual and group rights. These are important principles, and maintaining them in the context of a unified Iraq will be a demanding task.

In a March 6, 2002, press conference, President Bush was more explicit, indicating his support for an Iraqi federation (though he did not provide details).

Recommendations
- *The Bush administration should support a political constituting process that is broadly representative and has a high degree of international legitimacy.* The Task Force appreciates that the choice of Iraqi participants in a constitutional drafting exercise and a consultative process leading to a political transition will not necessarily be the result of democratic elections. To ensure broad domestic and international endorsement of the process, the Task Force recommends that the United Nations be given responsibility for organizing (with U.S. involvement and assistance) these consultative processes. The Task Force urges that strong efforts be made to include the involvement of Iraqi women, who have played an important role in socioeconomic and political issues in Iraq.

- *The Bush administration should encourage the development of a geographically based, federal system of government in Iraq.* In northern Iraq, the Kurdish population has operated outside of Ba'athist control for over a decade, and the administration should express support for substantial local control over local affairs in a future Iraq. While decisions on Iraq's constitutional structure should be made by Iraqis, the Task Force is concerned that a solution short of a federal system will risk conflict in a future Iraq. This perspective in support of a federal structure should be promoted by U.S. officials in their discussions with Iraqi counterparts and with Iraq's neighbors.

Background

Constabulary and police units can operate effectively only if they are supported by a transitional justice mechanism that ensures the continued and effective operation of other elements of the administration of justice, especially the courts. Iraq's judicial system will require an overhaul, as the 1968 Ba'athist constitution eliminated separation of powers, made civilian courts subservient to military courts, and created special courts that were not part of the regular judicial system. At the same time, coalition forces and U.S. civilian personnel will have to work with existing judicial institutions, which include a civilian court system with a high court and at least seven civil and criminal courts of varying jurisdiction.

A number of specialists in post-conflict rule-of-law issues have urged the deployment of legal and judicial teams to assist in both post-conflict administration of justice and judicial reform.[8] While such teams could have authority to dispense justice in a transition period, they would also work with local officials to monitor local courts—which could continue to adjudicate non-sensitive cases. Judicial team members might include lawyers, judges, court administrators, corrections officers, trainers, and translators. Presumably, they could also work with the judicial council on issues relating to the appropriate law to apply at the outset of the occupation and thereafter.

Status of Planning

Indications are that the administration has begun to consider actively the deployment of legal and judicial teams but that the planning process, as of late February, was just getting underway.

Recommendation

Deploy legal and judicial teams and seek international involvement.
The Task Force encourages the administration to promote the post-

---

[8]Perito, "Establishing Post-Conflict Security," p. 25. As indicated in footnote 2, the administration has not yet announced its position on the applicable governing law for Iraq during a transition period, and a final decision on this issue should involve extensive consultation with Iraqis.

conflict deployment of legal and judicial teams as described above, to help address immediate and longer-term post-conflict justice issues, and recommends that U.S. officials seek to recruit other governments to support such efforts. To ensure the effectiveness of such teams, especially if they are to have executive authority, it will be essential to identify, and to articulate clearly, the basis of interim law.

Accountability for Grave Abuses of Human Rights

Background

The government of Saddam Hussein has been responsible for grave and systematic abuses of human rights, including the killings and disappearances of between 250,000 and 290,000 Iraqis over the past two decades. These include at least 100,000 people who are believed to have been killed during the Anfal campaign against the Kurds. The regime is also believed to have killed up to 5,000 Kurdish villagers in a chemical weapons attack in Halabja[9] and committed grave abuses during the occupation of Kuwait.

It is difficult to imagine a post-conflict Iraq in which there is no process of accountability for these atrocities. The simple magnitude of the violations demands that perpetrators be held accountable. Moreover, the many thousands of families who have been victimized by the regime will have high expectations about accountability, which, if frustrated, could result in disaffection, protest, and even instability.

The key questions involve the kinds of judicial institutions that will be established for these purposes, the nature of their jurisdiction, and the timing of their creation.

Some have argued that trials of those implicated in the most serious abuses would be far too great a burden on Iraqi judicial institutions in the process of reform and have instead urged the estab-

---

[9]The actual number of victims may range from 4,000 to 7,000. However, 5,000 deaths is the most widely cited estimate. See Human Rights Watch, "Whatever Happened to the Iraqi Kurds?" March 11, 1999, available at http://www.staging.hrw.org/reports/1991/IRAQ913.htm. Also see Kendal Nezan, "Saddam's Other Victims—The Kurds," *Washington Post,* January 20, 1991.

lishment of a special international tribunal for these purposes. Others have suggested a so-called mixed tribunal, with both international and Iraqi representation, modeled after the recently formed Special Court in Sierra Leone. The role of domestic Iraqi courts in addressing less significant abuses would be determined by the pace and effectiveness of reform of those indigenous institutions.

Iraqis will have to determine the breadth of the criminal accountability processes for human rights violations, especially as those with relatively limited culpability might have skills and abilities that would give them a role to play in the rebuilding of Iraq. With respect to timing, proponents of delaying an accountability process would argue that early action would encourage fear and resistance by the large numbers of Ba'ath Party officials and military officers who might otherwise cooperate with the United States and its coalition partners in the immediate aftermath of the conflict. Moreover, if the scope of the accountability exercise is unclear or ambiguous, even those with minimal culpability might harbor such fears and manifest resistance. On the other hand, failure to move quickly on the accountability issue risks the destruction of evidence and gives human rights abusers time to develop strategies to resist accountability.

Status of Planning
Statements by U.S. government officials suggest that the administration favors prosecution of a relatively small number of senior Iraqi officials before Iraqi tribunals, or mixed tribunals that might include participation of international jurists. Trials of other officials who are less culpable but still responsible for grave abuses would presumably take place in Iraqi courts, and U.S. officials have also indicated that they support a truth and reconciliation process for those who have relatively minimal culpability. In such a process, the individual implicated in abuses might avoid prosecution if he or she provided a full accounting of the crimes committed.

Recommendation
Act early on accountability, seek international involvement in the process, and ensure a key role for Iraqis. The Task Force

believes that accountability issues should be an early priority for the transitional administration. In addition, international involvement in the process, through either the creation of an international ad hoc tribunal or the development of a mixed tribunal, will enhance the prospects for success. A mixed tribunal would have the advantage of ensuring Iraqi participation. The Task Force notes that a truth and reconciliation process could be established concurrently with such a tribunal, as a complement to criminal accountability for those who bear greatest responsibility for serious abuses.

ECONOMIC ISSUES

The Oil Industry

Assessing the Challenge

There are enormous expectations that the Iraqi oil industry will generate revenues for economic reconstruction and development in the aftermath of conflict in Iraq. Such expectations are not without merit, as Iraq is believed to have oil deposits second only to those of Saudi Arabia. Iraq's proven reserves are estimated at 112.5 billion barrels, and probable and possible resources are believed to be about 220 billion barrels.[10] Currently, Iraq is estimated to have a production capacity of up to 2.8 million barrels of oil per day (mbd), although actual production for 2002 averaged only about 2 mbd. Shutting down of production during hostilities—even assuming no substantial damage to facilities—will likely lower Iraqi capacity to 2.7 mbd at most.

At present, Iraq consumes about .5 mbd of oil. Thus exports, initially, are unlikely to exceed 2.2 mbd and could decline as consumption growth in the early phase of reconstruction outpaces increased output. If Iraq were to build output rapidly to reach full current capacity, the price of a barrel of U.S. benchmark West Texas

---

[10]"Winning the Peace: Managing a Successful Transition in Iraq," Atlantic Council, January 2003, p. 8.

Intermediate grade crude oil would likely decline to the low $20 range. At that level, the export price for Iraqi crude oil would be around $18 per barrel, yielding an annual revenue potential on the order of $14 billion to $16 billion.

Under the UN Oil for Food Program, established by Security Council Resolution 986 as an exception to overall economic sanctions, 72 percent of oil revenue funds the humanitarian program, 25 percent is allocated to the UN Compensation Fund for war reparation payments, 2.2 percent covers UN administrative and operational costs for administering Oil for Food, and 0.8 percent goes to the weapons inspection program. Thus, even assuming shifts in the allocation of this revenue and an end to diversion of oil exports outside the UN program, a need to fund ongoing humanitarian and rehabilitation activities would likely limit the availability of oil revenue for reconstruction. Overcoming this limitation and generating significant new oil revenues for reconstruction from within Iraq is likely to require substantial increases in oil production.

However, the costs of such production increases will be significant, and significant additional production capacity will not come on line quickly. In fact, due to deteriorating infrastructure, Iraq has been losing production capacity in recent years, and the rehabilitation requirements of Iraqi oil fields are formidable. For example, restoring production to its 1977 peak of about 3.5 mbd would require investment of about $5 billion to $7 billion over two years. To achieve more significant increases—say, to 6 mbd by 2010—Iraq would need multiyear investments totaling over $20 billion. There are also annual operating costs of around $3 billion.

In seeking to address these issues, U.S. officials will need to carefully set boundaries on the nature of their involvement in the oil sector. How this resource is managed will have enormous implications for Iraq's future, and there are several factors that would seem to suggest active U.S. engagement. While Iraq's oil industry includes many professionals with great technical competence, those in positions of leadership in the oil sector are widely believed to be senior Ba'ath Party members or cronies of Saddam Hussein. In addition, in societies where oil has dominated the economy, revenue has often been badly mismanaged, enriching only the few.

In the case of Iraq, U.S. officials have an interest not only in promoting an equitable distribution of the resource but also in initially ensuring the continuation of the Oil for Food Program, which has sustained the population. However, the people of Iraq, and much of the international community, will resist any U.S. engagement that they believe represents an effort to assert control over the oil industry, especially if that engagement persists over time.

Specifically, U.S. officials will have to develop a posture on a range of important questions relating to control of the oil industry. These include

- How should decisions on contracts for equipment and oil-field rehabilitation be made?

- Who should consider the viability of executory contracts for development of oil fields (at least some of which have as a precondition the lifting of sanctions)?

- What will be required for transition, over time, from the Oil for Food Program to a transparent and accountable indigenous system to receive and disburse oil-related revenues?

Administration Actions
Much of the planning on the oil issue appears to be taking place in the Defense Department. U.S. and allied military forces will quickly occupy, control, and protect oil fields. With the involvement of the U.S. military, American and expatriate experts, and Iraqi technical personnel, the United States will then reportedly seek to ensure that oil production can be managed effectively in the immediate aftermath of the conflict. Issues relating to the legal framework of claims, the flow of funds, the role of the industry in national development, and other planning questions were still to be resolved as of late February. This was clearly reflected in a February statement by Undersecretary Feith, who said that "we do not have final decisions ... on exactly how we would organize the mechanism to produce and market the oil for the benefit of the people of Iraq." Feith went on to say that "it would be beneficial to have that done to the maximum extent possible by Iraqis—by a mechanism that would be international in nature and

show the world … that our intention is to be completely honest, transparent, and respectful of the … rights … the property rights, in particular, of the Iraqi state and people."

Recommendations
- *Emphasize publicly that the United States will respect and defend Iraqi ownership of the country's economic resources, especially oil, and that the proceeds from oil production and sales should benefit all of the people of Iraq.* The Task Force urges that these sentiments play a prominent role in U.S. public diplomacy in Iraq and throughout the Arab world.

- *Seek an internationally sanctioned legal framework to assure a reliable flow of Iraqi oil and to reserve to a future Iraqi government the determination of Iraq's general oil policy.* The Task Force notes that this recommendation is similar to one first made by the Council on Foreign Relations–Baker Institute Working Group on Post-Conflict Policy in Iraq.[11] The Task Force believes that the framework, which could be affirmed by a UN Security Council resolution, could establish the right of the government of Iraq to determine its long-term oil-development plan on the basis of its national priorities. With respect to the guidelines for executory contracts, U.S. officials would want to ensure that the legal framework helps to "even the playing field" for firms that were denied the opportunity to compete for contracts during the period of sanctions.

  The Task Force also recommends establishment of a decision-making oversight board with international and significant Iraqi participation to consider issues that must be addressed during a post-conflict transition period. The criteria for consideration of future oil development or exploration contracts should be designed to ensure that energy policy decisions that could be easily postponed should await the election of a post-transition government.

---

[11]See the Report of an Independent Working Group, "Guiding Principles for U.S. Post-Conflict Policy in Iraq," Council on Foreign Relations, 2003, available at http://www.cfr.org/pdf/Post-War_Iraq.pdf.

- *Sustain but modify the structure of the UN Oil for Food Program.* Ultimately, a sovereign Iraq is not likely to need to continue the Oil for Food Program. But in the aftermath of conflict, the basic structure of the program, subject to modifications to ensure its non-political and transparent character and possibly to expand its scope to permit additional import of essential items, would serve many essential objectives. In particular, it would ensure the continued delivery of food and other humanitarian assistance, as well as address the issue of compensation claims.

  U.S. officials should engage with both Iraqis and UN officials on how this program might be progressively modified over time. A forum for such engagement could be the oversight board described above.

- *Address the potential impact of regime change on Jordanian oil imports from Iraq.* The Iraqi regime has provided the government of Jordan with free and heavily discounted oil. It is unclear whether such arrangements would continue in the post-conflict environment. In view of Jordan's economic situation and its important role on regional and international security issues, the administration should make efforts to address Jordanian needs in this area.

Reconstruction

Background

A key goal for the reconstruction effort will be to revitalize the Iraqi economy, as an economy growing across sectors and regions of the country means more jobs, increased opportunities for entrepreneurs, and greater overall stability. But the challenge will be formidable, as the Iraqi economy is typified by distortions. Cronyistic structures have allowed monopolistic practices to flourish. Goods are in limited supply and available only to those few who can afford them. One's connections to the regime, rather than profession or skill set, have been the key determinant of income level. Revitalizing the economy will require breaking down these dysfunctional structures and creating incentives for production. These include generating competition, ensuring new firms have the opportunity to start up and have access to capital, and providing adequate protections against mafia-style intimidation tactics so that certain individuals will not gain or maintain their unfair monopolistic advantage.

These requirements will demand a large infusion of resources to address a number of key challenges, some of which are described below.

Demand failure. Given what we know about the Iraqi economy, goods are readily available—to those who can afford them. Unfortunately, most people, even skilled professionals, cannot. A reconstruction effort will need to focus on this problem early on. Priorities should include generating private employment, ensuring that public salaries are paid, and supporting public works programs to generate incomes for large numbers of people before the economy is ready to generate necessary levels of employment. Ideally, public works programs would address, but not be limited to, essential infrastructural needs.

Financial institutions. Access to capital will be critical for stimulating private-sector activity. Iraq at one time had a relatively sophisticated financial sector that has declined during the years of Saddam Hussein's rule. Banks will have to be reformed to make capital considerably more accessible to new or expanding businesses of all sizes. Prior to such reforms, a reconstruction program will have to identify alternative means of obtaining credit.

Agriculture. Between 25 and 35 percent of the Iraqi population relies on agriculture for their livelihoods. However, the sector is not in good shape, as food and agricultural production has declined by 40 percent since 1990. This is due in part to the regime's decision to drain the irrigated swampland in the south, and in part to the deterioration in incentive structures, with access to inputs (fertilizer, feed, etc.) largely limited to regime cronies. Revitalizing this sector will require identification of seed varieties and sources, incentives and capital to repair farm equipment, reconstruction of irrigation infrastructure so that the country's water resources can be effectively used, and equitable access to market opportunities, among other reform activities.

Infrastructural repair. Roads, communications, electricity, and water supply are priority infrastructural concerns and would be a logical focus of intensive activity. This would also be the case with schools and other public institutions that may be damaged and in need of reconstruction and repair.

Even assuming little war-related damage, these requirements are imposing. Estimates of reconstruction financing needs vary considerably. A widely cited study estimates the totals at between $25 billion and $100 billion over a multiyear period, though others have suggested even higher figures.[12] Some illustrative numbers indicate clearly that the multibillion-dollar figures are not unreasonable. For example, it is estimated that repairing and restoring Iraq's electrical-power grid to its pre-1990 level could cost as much as $20 billion and that short-term repairs for the oil industry will cost between $5 billion and $7 billion.

Iraq's reconstruction challenges will be compounded by nearly $400 billion in financial obligations that include between $62 billion and $130 billion in debt to commercial banks and governments, over $200 billion in both unsettled and resolved compensation claims submitted to the UN Compensation Commission, some $100 billion in reparations claims related to the Iran-Iraq War, and nearly $60 billion in pending contracts (which are mostly in the energy and telecommunications sectors).[13]

Status of Planning

As of late February, the foreign policy agencies of the U.S. government were working closely with the Office of Management and Budget to prepare for Congress a supplemental funding request. Although the overwhelming bulk of this multibillion-dollar pro-

---

[12]For more details, see William D. Nordhaus, "The Economic Consequences of a War with Iraq," pp. 51–88, in Carl Kaysen et al., *War with Iraq: Cost, Consequences, and Alternatives* (American Academy of Arts & Sciences, 2002).

[13]Frederick D. Barton and Bathsheba N. Crocker, "A Wiser Peace: An Action Strategy for a Post-Conflict Iraq," Center for Strategic and International Studies, January 2003, p. 23.

posal will likely be for U.S. combat and peace stabilization forces, reconstruction funding will also be part of the package. And while U.S. officials are reluctant to make multiyear commitments of funds given the hope and expectation that oil revenues will ultimately finance development, U.S. officials appear to appreciate that it would be imprudent to rely (or rely solely) on such revenues in the initial post-conflict period.

The supplemental request will also include monies for humanitarian assistance. Here again, requirements are uncertain.

Recommendations
- *Request $3 billion in reconstruction and humanitarian assistance to Iraq for one year, and make clear the United States will be prepared to make substantial additional contributions in the future.* This initial contribution would include $2.5 billion for reconstruction and $500 million for humanitarian aid. As mentioned, it is difficult to anticipate funding needs given uncertainties that include 1) the actual reconstruction requirements; 2) the impact of conflict on those requirements; 3) the pace at which oil revenues will increase over time; and 4) the role of other donors. At the same time, the administration is likely to submit its budget request shortly after a conflict begins and will have to decide upon a funding level in an environment of uncertainty. Thus, the Task Force believes that a reconstruction contribution of $3 billion to meet reconstruction and humanitarian needs would both demonstrate a credible U.S. commitment to reconstruction and ensure that initial funding is adequate. A significant portion of this total should be designated for quick-impact projects such as rehabilitation of basic services and short-term employment. We also believe that a $500 million commitment to humanitarian assistance efforts, which are already underfunded, is also appropriate. (However, if there are significant interruptions in the availability of Iraqi oil revenues for the Oil for Food Program, the figure for humanitarian assistance would need to be considerably higher.)
- *Organize a donors' conference on reconstruction in Iraq, involving the international financial institutions as well as*

major donor governments. The Task Force notes that the feasibility of this proposal, as well as the one that follows directly below, would be enhanced by a UN Security Council resolution that endorses the overall post-conflict transition and reconstruction exercise and envisions significant international involvement in the post-conflict transition process in Iraq.

- *Engage other governments in efforts to delay, limit, or eliminate Iraqi debt and related obligations.* Action on the more than $100 billion in Iraqi debt would primarily involve negotiations in the Paris Club and with the International Monetary Fund, and claims issues would primarily involve review in the UN Security Council.[14]

REGIONAL DIPLOMATIC AND SECURITY ISSUES

Background

There has been much discussion of the regional demonstration effect that might result from democratic development in Iraq. Whatever this impact may be, the Task Force supports efforts to encourage the rule of law and democracy in the Middle East and the Persian Gulf. Moreover, a more democratic Iraq could forge working or even cordial relations with the governments of Turkey, Jordan, Kuwait, and Saudi Arabia, as well as other neighboring states, and the political reform process could exert constructive pressures within the region.

Also of concern, however, is the impact of U.S. intervention, and the resulting transformation of the Iraqi military, on the regional military balance of power. Of course, any consideration of this issue must distinguish between the period of U.S. presence and the longer-term future. As long as U.S. troops are in Iraq, none of the states in the region is likely to take advantage of the downsizing of Iraq's military and the diminution of Iraqi power. At the same time, neighboring states, particularly Iran, will pay great atten-

---

[14]Barton and Crocker, "A Wiser Peace," p. 23.

tion to the inevitable restructuring that the U.S. government will impose on Iraq's military. That restructuring is likely to be significant, as Iraq's army is estimated to have about 375,000 troops, 2,200 main battle tanks, 3,700 other armored vehicles, and 2,400 major artillery weapons. In addition, Iraq is believed to have more than 300 combat aircraft,[15] though these and other estimates may change after a conflict. In any event, the numbers are large relative to the size of Iraq's population, and downsizing will support the U.S. objective of ensuring that Iraq is no longer a threat to its neighbors.

However, there is broad agreement that Iraq's territorial integrity should be safeguarded, and downsizing could diminish the self-defense capabilities of a future government. In short, the dilemma is that any future Iraqi army powerful enough to defend Iraq against Iran may also be strong enough to overrun Saudi Arabia and Kuwait. The Task Force recommendations below attempt to address this tension.

Finally, a number of regional analysts have argued that a U.S. and allied intervention in Iraq should be followed by an energetic, U.S.-led diplomatic effort on the Arab-Israeli dispute. The argument is based on two propositions: first, that the U.S. presence and role in Iraq will enhance U.S. influence generally and create opportunities for progress on Middle East–related issues; and second, that the United States will have an interest in demonstrating to Arab governments and the Arab people that Americans are committed to a just peace between the Israelis and the Palestinians.

Status of Planning
Although details of administration planning for the Iraqi armed forces have yet to be publicly disclosed, administration officials have reportedly spoken of dismantling and then reconstituting the Iraqi army. In late November 2002, an expert working group organized by the National Defense University at the behest of the Department of Defense made a recommendation to this effect,

---

[15]Anthony H. Cordesman, "If We Fight Iraq: Iraq and the Conventional Military Balance," Center for Strategic and International Studies, revised June 28, 2002, p. 1.

and also called for quick parole for low-ranking enemy prisoners of war captured on the battlefield, detention and interrogation for mid- to senior-ranking officers, and detention and interrogation of intelligence and security force personnel.

The expert group distinguished between regular Iraqi army units and those of the Republican Guard, noting that the standard army is "relatively apolitical and poorly prepared for war or peace," and that some of its members might be used for civil works and public order. While the group noted that selected elements of the Republican Guard might be included in a reconstituted Iraqi army, they recommended against such inclusion for elements of the Special Republican Guard. The group also recommended that current Iraqi intelligence and security forces not be part of a new military, and that a transformed military be smaller and in a non-offensive posture.

As of February, it appeared that the Pentagon Office of Reconstruction and Humanitarian Assistance would have responsibilities for Iraqi military restructuring. Preliminary thinking was that much of the planning work in this area might be undertaken by civilian contractors, though implementation could involve a much broader array of actors (including the United States and other governments, as well as international organizations).

Finally, the administration has addressed possible connections between Iraq and the Middle East peace process. In particular, officials have suggested that a successful U.S. intervention and a regime change in Iraq will have a positive impact on mitigating the Arab-Israeli conflict and restarting the peace process. They have argued that democratic development in Iraq could serve to encourage the Palestinians to reform their institutions, and choose new leaders to negotiate peace with Israel and govern the future Palestinian state. Administration officials also believe that putting an end to Iraq's payments to families of suicide bombers would be an important step in the war on terrorism. U.S. officials have indicated to officials in the region and elsewhere that they anticipate a broader U.S. effort in the Middle East following an Iraq intervention.

Recommendations

- *Consider a regional forum for discussion of security issues.* The Task Force believes that, even with the removal of the regime of Saddam Hussein, there are factors that create serious risks of instability in the post-conflict regional military balance. In particular, and as suggested above, an Iraqi military that does not pose a threat to Saudi Arabia or Kuwait could itself be vulnerable to Iran. Iran has also made clear it will seek to promote its interests in Iraq, and further involvement by Iran in the postwar environment could have implications for stability. The administration should strongly consider encouraging a security forum with states in the region that could address confidence-building measures and other issues, such as external security guarantees and nonproliferation. Such a forum might resemble the UN Afghanistan "six plus two" format, through the inclusion of Iraq's neighbors and a few other key states, and could be organized with the lead of the UN secretary-general.

- *Closely monitor the professionalization and restructuring of the military, including disarmament, demobilization, and reintegration (DDR).* While the Task Force appreciates that private contractors have played valuable roles in various aspects of peace stabilization, their performance has been uneven in the past. If contracts in this area are awarded to private-sector entities, they should be closely supervised, both in Washington and on the ground, by U.S. civilian and military personnel, who should ensure that restructuring programs include curricula relating to civilian control of the military and respect for human rights. The DDR process will be particularly important in Iraq, as a downsizing of the army will result in many thousands of young Iraqi men losing employment, with the concomitant risks for public security. A number of other governments and international organizations, including the World Bank and the United Nations, have devoted resources and have developed expertise on these issues. In addition to any use of private contractors, the administration should be actively engaging these institutions on support for DDR.

[45]

- *Initiate post-conflict action on the Middle East peace process.*
  The Task Force encourages the administration to give high priority to an active post-conflict effort to engage the peace process as defined by the evolving "road map" developed by the Quartet—the United States, the European Union, Russia, and the United Nations. The Task Force believes that any such action by the Bush administration must be accompanied by greater efforts by Arab states and the Palestinian leadership to discourage and condemn acts of terrorism and violence against Israelis and elsewhere in the region.

CONCLUSION

Few question the importance of active U.S. engagement in peace stabilization and reconstruction in Iraq. In that country and throughout the region, the United States has vital and enduring interests relating to weapons of mass destruction, international terrorism, regional security, and respect for human rights, and the success of the political transition process in Iraq will have a substantial impact on America's ability to pursue its objectives effectively in the region. However, recent history has demonstrated that post-conflict peace-building can be an extremely complex challenge. In Iraq—where U.S. efforts will inevitably involve uncertainty, trial and error, and uneven progress—U.S. success will depend on America's determination to stay the course. In particular, the United States must sustain a long-term and substantial commitment of American resources and personnel, ensure the active involvement of other states and international organizations in post-conflict reconstruction, and promote participation by the people of Iraq in a process that validates their expectations about political reconciliation, a democratic transformation, and a more hopeful future.

ADDITIONAL OR DISSENTING VIEWS

The study's recommendations for reconstruction and humanitarian assistance to be provided by the United States in my view are exceedingly low. They are on a par with amounts pledged by the entire international donors' community for Afghanistan. As is often the case in these pledging sessions, it was easier to make a pledge to support Afghanistan than to collect the needed resources. Iraq, a larger, more complex nation, will constitute an even more difficult challenge and the United States, especially if it uses force without UN authorization, is much less likely to gain the support of other nations for the post-conflict stage.

J. Brian Atwood

The United States can win the war with Iraq alone, or at the head of a narrow coalition. It can win the peace, however, only with much broader backing. The price of policing Iraq, holding it together, reconstructing its economy, and reforming its society goes beyond anything the American taxpayer will or should be ready to bear.

Given currently limited international backing for war, the Bush administration has little option but to plan for a nationally led American post-conflict administration, as it is doing. But the perpetuation of such an arrangement beyond the first few weeks should be America's least favored option, not its most. As this report urges, the United States should move as quickly as possible to associate the United Nations and other international institutions with the process of forming a new Iraqi government, writing a new Iraqi constitution, holding free elections, and reforming the Iraqi economy.

Even in the area of security, where unity of command and American leadership is most essential, the United States should seek the early and substantial involvement of the North Atlantic Treaty Organization (NATO), an organization that has performed just such tasks preeminently well in the Balkans.

This report is right to highlight the open-ended nature of the peacekeeping commitment in Iraq. Even the lowest suggested requirement, for 75,000 troops, will require that every infantryman in the U.S. Army spend six months in Iraq out of every eighteen to twenty-four. Given other demands on U.S. forces, this is not a commitment America alone can long sustain. Nor can our current coalition partners, with the exception of the United Kingdom, provide much help.

In the late 1990s, first in Bosnia and then in Kosovo, the Russian government vehemently opposed NATO's use of force. In both cases, as soon as the fighting ceased, Russia then turned around and sent units to join the NATO forces sent to enforce the peace. Throughout this period, whenever strains with Russia were at their highest, the Clinton administration made every effort to salve wounded Russian pride, ignore its outbreaks of temper, and make clear that whatever the current differences, a future partnership was on offer. In the coming weeks the United States should put at least as much effort into mending fences with its closest allies as it did earlier with a former adversary. This means eschewing hyperbole about the death of NATO or the end of the UN, and instead laboring to make both institutions more relevant to the peace than they may have been to the war.

The report understates, if anything, the requirements for U.S. humanitarian and reconstruction assistance of $3 billion in the first year. Tiny Kosovo, a place twelve times less populous than Iraq, received nearly $1 billion in American aid in that time frame. And in the Balkans, Europe provided the lion's share of reconstruction assistance.

The partisan debate over nation-building is over. Administrations of both parties are clearly prepared to use American military forces to reform rogue states and repair broken societies. In the late 1940s, when the United States produced 50 percent of the world's gross national product (GNP), it was able to perform those tasks more or less on its own. In the 1990s, in the aftermath of the Cold War, America was able to lead much broader coalitions and thereby share the burden of nation-building much more widely. The United States cannot afford and does not need to go it alone in building a free Iraq. It will secure broader participation, however, only if it pays attention to the lessons of the 1990s as well as those of the 1940s.

James F. Dobbins

While I concede that it is impossible to place time frames on the progress of conflict and post-conflict developments, I am especially concerned that the report has no time frame, nor any indication of benchmarks, for the evolution of an Iraqi authority.

Although the report does not explicitly preclude the possibility of an Iraqi interim authority early in the transition process (and prior to elections), it should have made very clear that failure to establish an Iraqi-led authority early on in the process of transition would be a grave mistake for the United States, leave a dangerous political vacuum, and create ill feeling in Iraq and in the region, with incalculable consequences. Moreover, the absence of such an interim authority is not workable, because an empowered party has to enter into long-term planning for the country, including negotiation with the UN and with Iraq's creditors, and awarding the multiyear, multibillion-dollar contracts needed for electricity, communications, the oil industry, and so on. Only an Iraqi entity can do this.

It is not enough for Iraqis to be advisers and administrators. Within a few months of the end of conflict, Iraq must have a governing authority that fills the political vacuum during the transitional period and works alongside U.S. and international personnel. This authority, which should represent Iraqi national unity and Iraq's political and social diversity, must take shape in the early days, when the United States is still solidly on the ground and fully engaged, and able to provide breathing space and assistance for Iraqis to work out problems and differences.

Rend R. Francke

While I agree with the report's caution against imposing the external opposition as an interim governing authority, it cannot be emphasized too strongly that the United States must devolve power as quickly as possible to a national interim administration that is regionally and ethnically inclusive. While the United States is likely to be welcomed during the initial stages of the campaign, it is also likely to be challenged by internal forces backed by neighboring powers. An Iraqi authority needs to take responsibility at the earliest possible date for countering such forces and maintaining national cohesion.

Carl Gershman

While there is much in this report that is essential for the United States to implement if a post-Saddam exercise in state-building is to succeed, I am troubled by what I see as a lack of clarity about who is the ultimate arbiter in the process—the United States or the United Nations. Absolute clarity is required on this point if the Iraqi transition is to prove successful. Though recommendation #3 regarding burden-sharing for a post-conflict transition is necessary,[16] by giving the UN even titular control over activities such as leading the "political constituting process" for a new Iraqi government and establishing an oil oversight board, a dangerous myth is perpetuated.

The report skirts the critical point that UN international "control" over both the oil and constitutional questions would be a mere fig leaf to make American leadership more palatable. But this is not clever nuance; it fosters the myth that it is the UN, and not the United States and a coalition of the willing, that will reconstitute Iraq and much else in the world. This lack of clarity will lead to a failure to see where ultimate authority lies in the process, endangering the unity of command that is so essential to efforts to establish a self-sustaining post-war Iraq.

There is a fundamental objection to recommendation #3. Given the last six months, it is far from clear as to whether the UN Security Council would be amenable to UN resolutions endorsing American control over security and civil administration in the post-Saddam Iraq process; nowhere does it say in the report that the United States ought not to compromise on central issues involved in the state-building process and indeed *reserves the right*

---

[16]This number refers to a recommendation in the Executive Summary.

to move ahead with a coalition of the willing if the UN process bogs down. Having failed to thwart American security aims before the war, one does not get to hamstring U.S. efforts to transform Iraq after the fighting. While I am fully committed to signing the Task Force report, I can only do so with this vital exception.

John C. Hulsman

Should a war occur in Iraq, it is imperative that the United States and the international community deal with its aftermath as effectively as possible. That is the basis of my participation in this Task Force, whose product should be taken very seriously by the Bush administration.

At the same time, and understanding that participation in the Task Force does not imply support for the use of force against Iraq, I must point out that the report puts me in the uncomfortable position of telling the U.S. administration how to do better what, in my opinion, it ought not to be doing at all. As I have indicated elsewhere, the administration has taken upon itself a task (changing the Iraqi regime) for which it has no mandate, invoking a goal (remaking the Middle East) for which it is unqualified, by invoking a rationale (that Iraq presents a threat to U.S. national security that cannot be contained or deterred by means other than war) that it has yet to demonstrate.

Nonetheless, given the likelihood of war, the report serves a valuable function, and many of its recommendations are of vital importance, in particular those relating to the protection of Iraqi civilians and to the need to internationalize administration of post-conflict Iraq (though again, it is difficult to separate this latter issue from the lack of international support for this war). Of particular importance is the report's emphasis on the role that the Iraqi people themselves, including many working for the current regime, must play in the process.

A final word about the broader regional context. The report urges the administration to engage in the Middle East peace process but then weakens its call by equating any future effort with the Quartet's road map. I strongly believe that the United States ought to be far more deeply and actively involved in seeking to end the current confrontation. But the road map, at least as currently defined, is not up to the task. Genuine pressure needs to be placed on both sides, Palestinian and Israeli, to end the violence and actions that contribute to its recurrence and to move to end their conflict in a manner that meets both sides' vital needs. U.S. leadership in forging an international coalition to promote that goal is long overdue.

If a military confrontation with Iraq were to serve that cause, it would at least mitigate the heavy costs of an ill-conceived war.

Robert Malley

Given the likelihood of imminent U.S. intervention in Iraq, even those who oppose key elements of U.S. policy must grapple with the formidable responsibilities that will confront America in the wake of war. Although I do not agree with all of the conclusions of this report, I believe that the Task Force makes invaluable contributions, most notably by directing attention to the security of Iraqi civilians.

I am nonetheless concerned that, by taking current administration policy as its point of departure, the report may inadvertently cross the line from realistic anticipation of likely developments to acceptance of that policy as a fait accompli. At a time when diplomatic efforts to define a broadly accepted policy on Iraq are in high gear, it would be unfortunate for this Task Force to imply, however inadvertently, that the most controversial features of U.S. policy cannot be recast to respond to legitimate questions raised by other countries and the American public.

After effectively mobilizing a robust response to Iraq's defiance of its disarmament obligations, the Bush administration has imperiled our ability to confront the Iraqi threat, as well as America's strategic effectiveness across a range of issues, by needlessly straining core alliances. The unfortunate result has been to divert attention from the threat posed by Iraq to apprehensions about the perceived perils of unconstrained U.S. power. In this context, the United States should redouble its efforts to find common ground with allies who remain unconvinced that war is urgently necessary but are open to persuasion about the most effective way to meet the Iraqi challenge.

These concerns have direct bearing on the subject of this report. For if military intervention is all but inevitable, our ability to win the proverbial peace will be profoundly affected by how and why a U.S.-led coalition goes to war.

Diane F. Orentlicher

TASK FORCE MEMBERS

J. BRIAN ATWOOD* is Dean of the Humphrey Institute of Public Affairs at the University of Minnesota. He served as the Administrator of the U.S. Agency for International Development during the Clinton administration.

KENNETH H. BACON is the President and CEO of Refugees International. Between 1994 and 2001, he served as the Assistant Secretary of Defense for Public Affairs and Pentagon spokesperson.

EDWARD P. DJEREJIAN is the founding Director of the James A. Baker III Institute for Public Policy at Rice University. He served as the U.S. Ambassador to Syria and Israel and was Assistant Secretary of State for Near Eastern Affairs between 1991 and 1993.

JAMES F. DOBBINS* is the Director of the Rand Corporation Center for International Security and Defense Policy. He was Ambassador to the European Community (1991–1993), Special Assistant to the President for the Western Hemisphere (1996–1999), and Assistant Secretary of State for Europe (2001–2002). He served as the Clinton administration's special envoy for Somalia, Haiti, Bosnia, and Kosovo, and most recently as the Bush administration's special envoy for Afghanistan.

STANLEY FISCHER is the Vice Chairman of Citigroup and the President of Citigroup International. He served as the First Deputy Managing Director of the International Monetary Fund from September 1994 to August 2001, and as Special Adviser to the Managing Director from September 2001 until January 2002.

Note: Task Force members participate in their individual and not institutional capacities.
*Individual largely concurs with the statement but submitted an additional view or a dissenting view.

Task Force Members

REND R. FRANCKE* is Executive Director of the Iraq Foundation. She has written extensively on Iraqi politics and is the coauthor of *The Arab Shia: The Forgotten Muslims*, published in 2000.

BART FRIEDMAN is a Senior Partner at Cahill Gordon & Reindel and serves on the Brookings Institution's Board of Trustees.

CARL GERSHMAN* has been the President of the National Endowment for Democracy since 1984.

JOHN C. HULSMAN* is a Research Fellow in European Affairs at the Davis Institute for International Studies at the Heritage Foundation. He also served as a Fellow in European Studies at the Center for Strategic and International Studies in Washington and taught world politics and U.S foreign policy at the University of St. Andrews, in Scotland.

JEANE J. KIRKPATRICK is a Senior Fellow at the American Enterprise Institute and Professor Emeritus at Georgetown University. She served as U.S. Permanent Representative to the United Nations during the Reagan administration and was a member of President Reagan's cabinet and National Security Council.

ELLEN LAIPSON is President and CEO of the Henry L. Stimson Center. She worked on U.S. policy toward Iraq in the 1990s at the National Intelligence Council, the National Security Council, and the U.S. Mission to the United Nations. She served as Vice Chair of the National Intelligence Council from 1997 to 2002.

ROBERT MALLEY* is the Director of the International Crisis Group's Middle East Program. He served on the National Security Council staff from 1994 to 2001, where his final position was as Special Assistant to the President for Arab-Israeli Affairs.

PHEBE MARR is a leading specialist on Iraq and was a Senior Fellow at the National Defense University.

EDWARD L. MORSE is Senior Executive Adviser at Hess Energy Trading.

GREGORY S. NEWBOLD is the Executive Vice President and Chief Operating Officer of the Potomac Institute for Policy Studies. A retired Lieutenant General, he was formerly the Director of Operations on the Joint Staff.

DIANE F. ORENTLICHER* is Professor of International Law at American University's Washington College of Law.

THOMAS R. PICKERING, co-chair of the Task Force, is Senior Vice President for International Relations at Boeing. His diplomatic career spanned five decades and included service as the U.S. Permanent Representative to the United Nations. He retired from government in 2001 as Undersecretary of State for Political Affairs.

JAMES A. PLACKE is a Senior Associate at Cambridge Energy Research Associates (CERA) and a nonresident Senior Fellow at the Brookings Institution. Previously he was Director for Middle East Research at CERA.

KENNETH M. POLLACK is a Senior Fellow in Foreign Policy Studies and Director of Research at the Brookings Institution's Saban Center for Middle East Policy. He served as Director for Persian Gulf Affairs at the National Security Council from 1999 to 2001.

JAMES R. SCHLESINGER, co-chair of the Task Force, is the Chairman of the MITRE Corporation's Board of Trustees and Senior Adviser at Lehman Brothers. He is also Counselor and Trustee for the Center for Strategic and International Studies and Chairman of the Executive Committee at the Nixon Center. He served as Secretary of Defense and Secretary of Energy.

Note: Individual largely concurs with the statement but submitted an additional view or a dissenting view.

Task Force Members

ERIC P. SCHWARTZ, director of the Task Force, is a Senior Fellow at the Council on Foreign Relations. He served on the National Security Council staff from 1993 to 2001, where he finished his tenure as Special Assistant to the President for National Security Affairs and Senior Director for Multilateral and Humanitarian Affairs.

JOHN M. SHALIKASHVILI is a Visiting Professor with the Institute for International Studies at Stanford University. After the 1991 Gulf War, he commanded Operation Provide Comfort, the international mission that provided humanitarian assistance and protection to Kurds in northern Iraq. He retired from the U.S. Army in 1997, after serving as Chairman of the Joint Chiefs of Staff.

RICHARD H. SOLOMON is President of the United States Institute of Peace. He formerly served as Assistant Secretary of State for East Asian and Pacific Affairs from 1989 to 1992.

GORDON R. SULLIVAN is the President and Chief Operating Officer of the Association of the United States Army (AUSA). He served as co-chair of the Commission on Post-Conflict Reconstruction, a joint project of the Center for Strategic and International Studies and AUSA. He retired from the U.S. Army in 1995, after serving as the Army's 32nd Chief of Staff.

FRANK G. WISNER is Vice Chairman of External Affairs at American International Group, Inc. Ambassador Wisner has served in a number of senior positions in the U.S. government, including Undersecretary of Defense for Policy from 1993 to 1994, and Undersecretary of State for International Security Affairs from 1992 to 1993.

TASK FORCE OBSERVERS

RACHEL BRONSON
Council on Foreign Relations

WENDY CHAMBERLIN
U.S. Agency for International Development

ROBERT M. DANIN
U.S. Department of State

SCOTT R. FEIL
Alion Science and Technology

DAVID L. GOLDWYN
Goldwyn International Strategies, LLC

ARTHUR C. HELTON
Council on Foreign Relations

PAUL D. HUGHES
U.S. Department of Defense

JUDITH KIPPER
Council on Foreign Relations

LAITH KUBBA
National Endowment for Democracy

RICHARD W. MURPHY
Council on Foreign Relations

ANDREW PARASILITI
Office of Senator Chuck Hagel

Task Force Observers

DAVID L. PHILLIPS
Council on Foreign Relations

ROBIN ROIZMAN
Office of Representative Tom Lantos

DENNIS SABAL
U.S. Department of Defense

JAMES A. SCHEAR
National Defense University

ANITA SHARMA
Woodrow Wilson International Center for Scholars

JOSEPH SIEGLE
Council on Foreign Relations

PUNEET TALWAR
Office of Senator Joseph R. Biden

OTHER REPORTS OF INDEPENDENT TASK FORCES
SPONSORED BY THE COUNCIL ON FOREIGN RELATIONS

* †*America–Still Unprepared, Still in Danger* (2002)
   Gary Hart and Warren B. Rudman, Co-Chairs; Stephen E. Flynn, Project
   Director
* †*Threats to Democracy* (2002)
   Madeleine K. Albright and Bronislaw Geremek, Co-Chairs; Morton H.
   Halperin, Project Director; Elizabeth Frawley Bagley, Associate Director
* †*Balkans 2010* (2002)
   Edward C. Meyer, Chair; William L. Nash, Project Director
* †*Terrorist Financing* (2002)
   Maurice R. Greenberg, Chair; William F. Wechsler and Lee S. Wolosky,
   Project Co-Directors
* †*Enhancing U.S. Leadership at the United Nations* (2002)
   David Dreier and Lee H. Hamilton, Co-Chairs; Lee Feinstein and Adrian
   Karatnycky, Project Co-Directors; Cosponsored with Freedom House
* †*Testing North Korea: The Next Stage in U.S. and ROK Policy* (2001)
   Morton I. Abramowitz and James T. Laney, Co-Chairs; Robert A. Manning,
   Project Director
* †*The United States and Southeast Asia: A Policy Agenda for the New
   Administration* (2001)
   J. Robert Kerrey, Chair; Robert A. Manning, Project Director
* †*Strategic Energy Policy: Challenges for the 21st Century* (2001)
   Edward L. Morse, Chair; Amy Myers Jaffe, Project Director
* †*State Department Reform* (2001)
   Frank C. Carlucci, Chair; Ian J. Brzezinski, Project Coordinator;
   Cosponsored with the Center for Strategic and International Studies
* †*U.S.-Cuban Relations in the 21st Century: A Follow-on Report* (2001)
   Bernard W. Aronson and William D. Rogers, Co-Chairs; Julia Sweig and
   Walter Mead, Project Directors
   †*A Letter to the President and a Memorandum on U.S. Policy Toward Brazil*
   (2001)
   Stephen Robert, Chair; Kenneth Maxwell, Project Director
* †*Toward Greater Peace and Security in Colombia* (2000)
   Bob Graham and Brent Scowcroft, Co-Chairs; Michael Shifter, Project
   Director; Cosponsored with the Inter-American Dialogue
   †*Future Directions for U.S. Economic Policy Toward Japan* (2000)
   Laura D'Andrea Tyson, Chair; M. Diana Helweg Newton, Project Director
* †*Promoting Sustainable Economies in the Balkans* (2000)
   Steven Rattner, Chair; Michael B.G. Froman, Project Director
* †*Nonlethal Technologies: Progress and Prospects* (1999)
   Richard L. Garwin, Chair; W. Montague Winfield, Project Director
* †*U.S. Policy Toward North Korea: Next Steps* (1999)
   Morton I. Abramowitz and James T. Laney, Co-Chairs; Michael J. Green,
   Project Director
   †*Safeguarding Prosperity in a Global Financial System: The Future Interna-
   tional Financial Architecture* (1999)
   Carla A. Hills and Peter G. Peterson, Co-Chairs; Morris Goldstein, Project
   Director
* †*Strengthening Palestinian Public Institutions* (1999)
   Michael Rocard, Chair; Henry Siegman, Project Director
* †*U.S. Policy Toward Northeastern Europe* (1999)
   Zbigniew Brzezinski, Chair; F. Stephen Larrabee, Project Director
* †*The Future of Transatlantic Relations* (1999)
   Robert D. Blackwill, Chair and Project Director

---

†Available on the Council on Foreign Relations website at http://www.cfr.org.
*Available from Brookings Institution Press. To order, call 1-800-275-1447.